Just Wondering

David Brodie

published by
Smilite Ltd

ISBN: 9781 7396 515 41

What do you think? Does what you think make any difference in the world? Do you think much at all?

This book is for provoking discussion, and provoking thought.

It does not provide 'all the answers'. In fact anyone who claims to have **all** the answers can only be described as a liar – a confidence trickster.

Of course, some people will approach discussion as something that must be 'won' – a competition. They hope that by winning an argument they will gain social standing in their group, and they will feel better about theselves. They, too, are dishonest.

Truth is elusive, which gives plenty of space in which the dishonest can play.

Does truth exist at all? It's difficult, perhaps impossible, to achieve perfect truth. But perhaps it is an ideal that we can try to appoach as closely as we can. That could mean that it is worth putting the search for truth, however imperfect it may be, ahead of short-term self-promotion. Ahead of personal greed. Ahead of deception. Ahead of bullying. Ahead of cruelty.

Contents

What's real? Who's real?   Finding reliable knowledge   page 4

Me, me, me (and everybody else)   Egocentrism   page 16

Who are you kidding?   Truth and lies   page 32

Us and them   Cultural centrism   page 38

Us and not-us   Anthropo centrism   page 50

Jumping right in or stepping right back   Two ways of seeing the world   page 60

The big us and the big not-us   So just how important are we? (Part one) page 70

Are we at the centre of everything?   So just how important are we? (Part two) page 78

Models of everything   Picture thinking   page 88

Awe and wonder   We don't have all the answers   page 92

Glossary   page 94

Image credits   page 100

This is not an apple.

It's not an apple. It's much more likely to be a two-dimensional representation (an image) that triggers the idea of the fruit. The sense of the picture and the sense of an apple exist inside your head.

If all your sensations are inside your head then is there even a real picture in the space outside of you?

Or is your mind the entire universe, containing pictures, apples, your right thumb, next door's cat, galaxies, and this book? Are you nothing more or less than an amazing imagination?

Where are you aware of other people? Only inside your head. So do you create them all, and are you the only one that exists?

They might seem like silly questions. But it's quite hard to prove, with absolute certainty, that what happens inside your mind is connected to a real outside world.

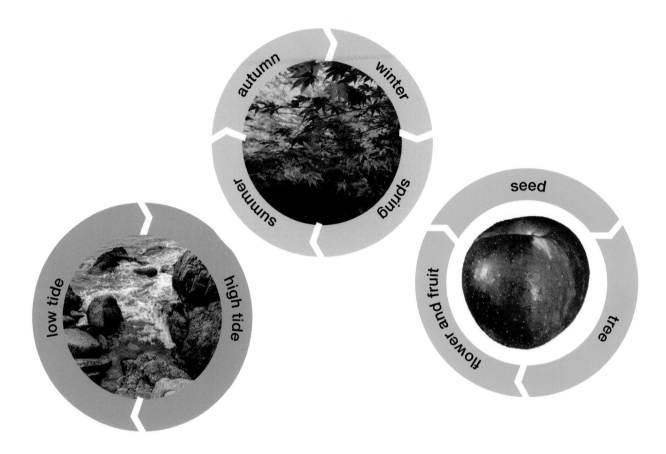

We sense changes – the tides on the ocean, the seasons of the year, the growth of apple trees and apples, the human body's development into adulthood, followed by personal aging and death. Do changes like these, that we are unable to control, exist only in our minds?

Perhaps if we don't seem to be in control of all our experiences then that suggests that they are outside our selves. It seems likely. It seems like 'common sense', but is common sense right every time? Absolute proof is hard to find.

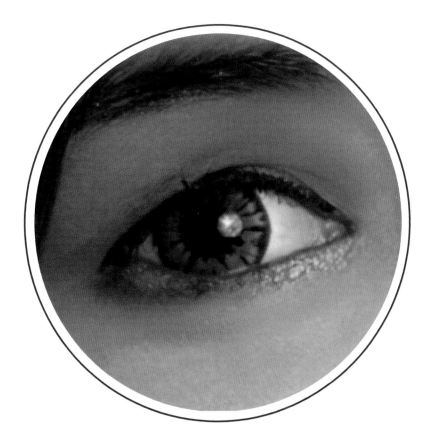

The idea that there is no reality outside your own mind has a name – solipsism. It is difficult, perhaps impossible, to completely and absolutely disprove the notion.

But still we believe that everyday 'visual sensation' arrives from an external world. Other sensations – sound, smell, taste, touch, including pain – also happen inside our heads, although we generally believe that they originate on the outside.

Dreams seem to have visual sensation. Maybe our brains (whatever they are – they are not something we see every day) go off on little rambles, pulling out assortments of memories, and mixing them into unfamiliar sequences. Or, just maybe, our dreams are the true reality inside our solitary selves.

experience   predictions

We can make predictions, based on previous 'inside our heads' senses, such as expectations of the good taste of an apple. When senses are repeated, predictably, we accumulate experiences. It seems that we learn to associate a particular taste experience with a biting-into-an-apple experience.

You can predict how a knife will behave when it's used to cut the fruit. You don't have to make a one-off guess about whether it's better to use the sharper edge of the blade. Your knowledge appears to be reliable enough to cut the apple, without cutting yourself, time after time.

Sensations inside our heads seem to build up over time. Apparently, we learn. If that is true, then this baby is learning to connect the 'inside world' with what is and what is not controllable and predictable in the 'world that seems to be on the outside'.

So it seems that every human learns how to predict the behaviour of objects 'out there', such as toys. There are also objects that are both 'out there' and 'in here' (connected directly to our heads) at the same time, like our own hands.

The consistency of the behaviour of the world, and our abilities in controlling some parts of it, but not all, make us pretty much convinced that there is something 'real' outside our own heads. The conviction comes from experience, not from step-by-step logical thinking.

If we let go of a ball ... we experience its fall. New-born babies don't know that is what to expect, but they learn. In fact we learn so well that we call it 'common sense', and we often suppose that it's too obvious to be worth thinking about. We become good at predicting how that 'outside world' behaves.

An important thing about predictions about the world is that you can test them. In experiments we can test predictions that are based on our existing ideas.

Imagine that jumping out of a plane is a kind of experiment. If your ideas about space, time, gravity, and the air resistance that makes parachutes work, are all wrong and you fall faster and faster then, in your final moments of fear, you will have the 'satisfaction' of discovering this.

Your discovery would change how most of us see the world, if only you could tell us instead of just screaming.

If you survive the experience then that supports your ideas. However, it doesn't prove absolutely that your ideas about time, space, gravity and parachutes are all absolutely correct – there could, just perhaps, be some other explanation for your nice gentle landing back on the ground.

11

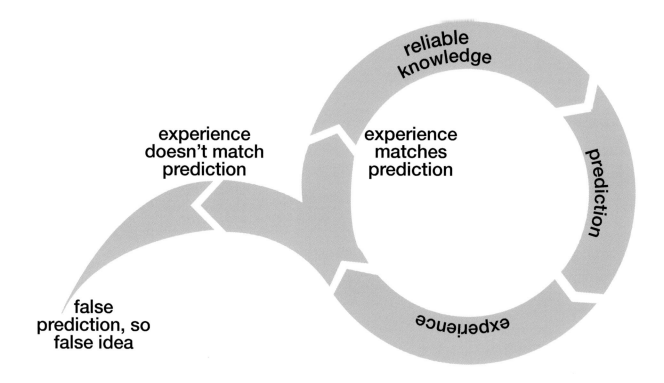

reliable knowledge

prediction

experience

experience matches prediction

experience doesn't match prediction

false prediction, so false idea

Predictions, followed by experience to try them out, can produce 'reliable' but not absolutely certain knowledge.

If the new experience matches the prediction ... it doesn't prove anything ... it could be fluke. But if we repeat the process over and over, and we find that the predictions always work out, then sooner or later we can conclude that we have reliable knowledge. It's how we check scientific knowledge. Which means that good scientific knowledge is reliable, very reliable, so far, rather than absolutely certain.

Another name for this reliable knowledge is provisional knowledge. We believe it to be true ... provided that the next experiment doesn't show it to be false.

She's making predictions, without consciously thinking about them. She's probably tested those unconscious predictions many times, by the experience of falling off more than once before she sharpened her predictive ability.

We make and test predictions in everyday life, as well as in science. We get to know when knowledge is strong enough to be treated as truth – reliable knowledge – reliable enough for safety when skateboarding, parachuting, and crossing the road.

13

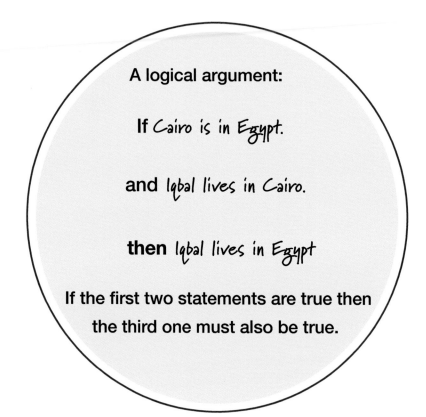

A logical argument:

If Cairo is in Egypt.

and Iqbal lives in Cairo.

then Iqbal lives in Egypt

If the first two statements are true then the third one must also be true.

Sometimes by combining one statement with another we can reach a new 'logical' conclusion, with certainty ... as long as the first two statements are certainly true.

The argument still depends on the starting points – how do we KNOW that Iqbal lives in Cairo? Only from experience. So this example of use of logic is still of little use for offering absolute certainty about the big, wide world.

The existence of invisible atoms is reliable (or provisional) knowledge because it has been around the circle of prediction and tested by experience, many times. No prediction, so far, has ever shown that the idea is false. So it's OK to go ahead and build computers, develop medicines, study stars, and more, based on the 'knowledge' of atoms.

For knowledge based on experience, which is an awful lot of knowledge that we rely on every day, maybe we just need to abandon the notion of absolute certainty. We can recognise that this is not an ideal world, and just 'reliable, so far' is as good as it gets. That way we can escape from solipsism and behave as if there is a real world outside ourselves.

It's MY world and I'll scream if I want to.

Small children may sometimes throw tantrums when the world outside themselves, including parents and other children, is not as controllable as they would like.

Most children gradually learn social skills, recognising that there are others, who have interests of their own, and that while self-centeredness sometimes pays, self-interest is often best served by working together. There is a choice between 'grab that toy before anyone else gets it' and 'if you just grab you don't get many friends'.

And grabbers can easily become victims of grabbing. That encourages most people to learn that 'no grabbing' is the way to go.

Maybe that's how people become a complex blend of crude me-me-me selfishness and us-us-us collective behaviour.

16

Welcome to social life.

However hard it is to prove, for the sake of getting on with those 'seemingly-out-there-things' that we call 'other-people' we each have to suppose that our own self is not the entire Universe. It seems better to assume that other people are real, with minds of their own. Then we can say goodbye to the loneliness of solipsism and start to enjoy a 'real' social life.

Happy time ...

... candles will be blown out, and perhaps a wish will be made.

What happens next? Does one person grab all the cake and leave the others with nothing? Probably not. Children don't often do that at birthday parties. What about adults?

What if it's not about cake but about land, houses, money?

One person could be greedy, and grab more than a 'fair share'.

And what would happen if there were just one slice? Suppose that it is all the food that there is at the birthday party (which would make it a disappointing party, for sure). Also, suppose that the one slice is the only food that anybody has seen all day. All the party guests are hungry.

Then the issues become more complicated. Does everybody have the right to exercise self-interest? Should they do that by depriving others?

Is the world already one in which some people can grab more than others?

In a world of limited cake supply, is the 'grab-it-quick' approach inevitable, and is it something we should just get used to?

19

Mister Scrooge is a fictional character (in *A Christmas Carol*, by Charles Dickens), famous for loving nothing but money, and for being very mean. He didn't care about other people. He was egocentric.

You can be selfish sometimes (like everybody else), but unless you live in a complete isolation, then your selfishness must play out in a social environment where you must interact with other people.

To live 'social lives' it's normal to mature beyond egocentrism and recognise that other people have thoughts and feelings much like our own. Scrooge didn't much care for social life.

other people (and everything else)

me

egocentrism

Egocentrism is not the same as solipsism. Egocentric, or egotistic, behaviour is based on the idea that other people may exist but I am the important one. True egotists may see other people only as resources to be used.

Certainly people can be selfish. But are we all entirely selfish?

Do we just live entirely for ourselves? Or must we at least respect other people, if only because they can hurt us if we don't? Are we in fact happier if we go beyond a me-me-me attitude to life?

We have a word for the unpleasantness of isolation. Loneliness.

We live with other people, in families, for example, and in other groups of different sizes that we mix with in everyday life. Other people can be annoying sometimes, but in the end these communities seem to offer not just familiarity but a sense of security. Some people offer care, and in some cases that care goes far beyond an 'everyday' level and can be called love.

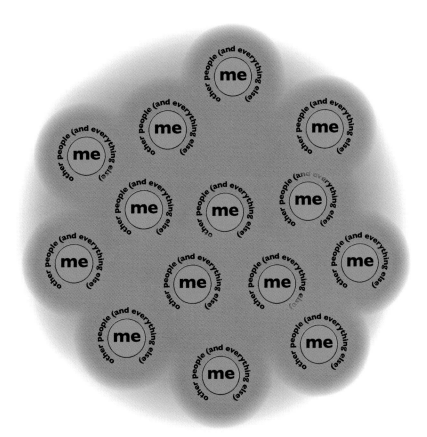

Each of us has time alone, and it can be good to have a little bit of private space. But we can't be happy in endless solitude, and on a practical level we can't cope on a day-to-day basis without food, water and more. We rely on others to supply a lot of what we need unless we grow all our own food, build our own shelter, have our own water supply and a hygienic system for getting rid of every kind of waste.

A me-centred philosophy that doesn't take account of our interdependence doesn't seem like a complete philosophy.

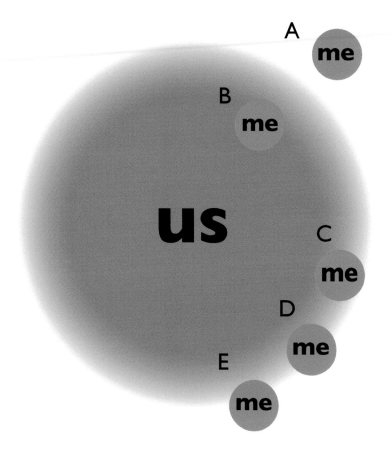

You know some of the people around you very well, and some you speak to only occasionally, or never.

Maybe you could try to be like A, completely separated from all other people. But how could a small child even learn to speak if she or he were isolated in this way?

Or you could be like B, snugly surrounded by others and never caring about personal space.

C, D and E show possibilities for being part of the 'us' but having some personal and private time as well.

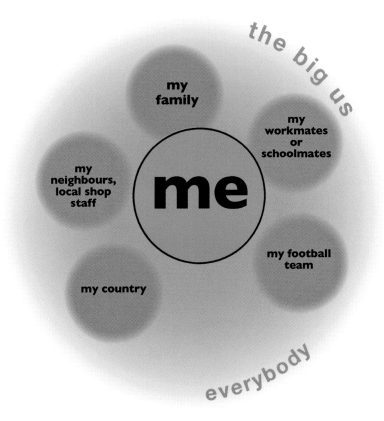

Let's clarify 'us'. There are many kinds. But the entire set, a whole planet full, could be called 'the big us'.

However, different people might have different ideas about the 'us' they belong to.

What is your first language? What kind of accent do you have? How did you come to speak with that accent? Do you feel part of one locality? Or one country? One religion? How? Why?

Do you feel part of the world's species that we call 'human'? And what about other species?

Every still picture you've ever seen – painting, photograph, or illustration in a book (like this one) – presents a limited view of the world. It misses out an important aspect – TIME.

Does that make static imagery pointless? Or do two-dimensional pictures at least give our thoughts some help so we can think about the world step-by-step?

In a complicated world our minds need all the help they can get, so to say 'the world is a bit, if not exactly, like this' can be useful. In language, such comparison of one thing with another might be called a metaphor. In science, a representation that is an aid to thinking about the world is a model. Several of the images in the book, such as the one on the facing page, could be called models.

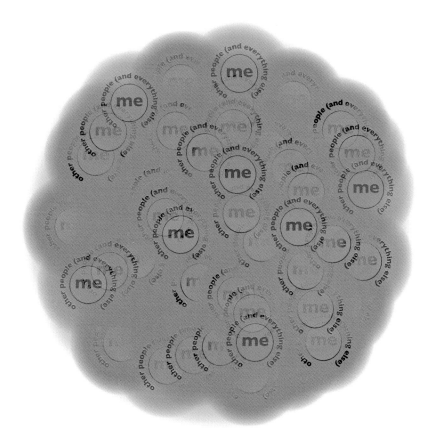

It's just a static model, but the blurry trails of me and me and me are intended to suggest movement. People do indeed move. And they sometimes step into the personal space of others.

'Personal space' could be the volume that our bodies physically occupy, plus a small region around us. It could also be used to mean our personal self-interests, including our personal well-being. Perhaps we should call that 'personal interest space'. Some people, egotists like Mr Scrooge, have little respect for the personal interests of others. Others are bullies, who actively push their way into the personal interest space of people around them.

Do each of us have the right to own our physical personal space and also to our personal interest space, but only if we respect the space of every other person? It's hard to justify if it works one way only.

She's selling. She grows some things herself, but she buys most of her produce from a wholesale seller, and in turn she offers them to anybody who visits her stall.

And, so, she makes a living, as long as she can buy at a cheaper price than $3.99 for a dozen eggs, 99 cents for a lemon, and so on ... and then can sell enough.

Is she selfish? If she were completely unselfish she would give food away, for free. But then how would she buy the fruit, vegetables and eggs for her market stall? And she'd have no money to pay her bills – it seems unreasonable to expect that level of unselfishness.

She's also buying and selling. She's trading in shares of businesses, and she wants to buy at a lower price and sell higher. So she's watching fluctuations in the state of various companies, and of the average of all companies. If she gets it right she can make a lot of money, but if she is not careful, or if she is unlucky, she can lose money. Maybe she is trading for herself, using her own money. Or maybe she works for a bank, or a pension fund ... and if so then she will be well paid.

She buys and sells businesses, and those may have many employees, who do the necessary work. Many of those employees won't be well paid. Is she selfish, for making money from the work of others? If the process is carefully controlled by good laws then can the benefits can be shared by society in general? Can self-interest, controlled by laws, be a good thing?

What's the best way of improving life in your local community, your district, your country, and for yourself? What's the best way of breaking down traditional inequalities? How about education?

Many people believe in the value of education. Some people are more reluctant, and the reasons for that are interesting. Is it just laziness that stops people making progress? Is it that some learners are better than others at working now for a reward later? (Psychologists give a name to that phenomenon – deferred [that is, 'can happen later'] gratification [pleasure or reward].)

Or is it that, in the face of old inequalities, some families feel alienated by the process of education (so that they actually allow those inequalities to persist)?

In the end, while there is money then some people are likely to have more than others.

In a truly moral society, should all children have the same opportunity at the start of life? This is not often the case.

In many places there are traditional views that some people are innately superior to others, even before they are born. Such layers of status produce a class system, or a 'caste' system. Traditions like that don't change easily, and some people may even feel proud of the cultural identity ('this is OUR way of doing things') that goes with a built-in social hierarchy.

Societies can be layered by money, by tradition, or by a mixture of those. Either way, in such societies some people are reckoned to be better than others from the moment they are born.

Beware! Deceit is part of human life. People tell lies. Some liars act alone, but there can be group lies, too.

And are we always completely honest with ourselves? Our daydreams, our hopes for the future can often be delusions. How we understand ourselves can be too optimistic – as in 'I am the best and most important person in the world' – or too negative – as in 'I am hopeless at everything'. It's very unlikely that either of those is true.

You see an ad on TV – with people who are judged to be 'beautiful', on a gorgeous beach, eating ice creams that look sooo delicious. You want to be having fun with them on that beach. So you buy one of those 'magical' ice creams. But your life doesn't change. The advertisers have deluded you, and you walked right in to the delusion. They've got you sussed, those advertisers.

How people place trust, and don't place trust, is strange. The decision tends to be an emotional one and not one that is much thought about.

So although people count their change when they go shopping, they easily trust political leaders who know when and how to smile, when and how to frown, and most importantly know how give an impression of confidence. It's not hard for evil people to hold great power.

Many people will follow bad leaders simply so that they don't have to think too hard for themselves. They allow others to do their thinking for them. These are behaviours that are found all over the world.

Human group behaviour is as important as our patterns of one-by-one behaviour.

Some individuals can work a crowd. They can get people on their side, and even stir their audience up into a state of near-euphoria. They might do it to sell something. They might do it because they themselves find it thrilling – they love to be loved by the crowd.

Or they might do it to gain power. That is, they might do it to get votes. In that case they might have little respect for the people they are winding up. ("Winding them up into a state of excitement was just too easy. What fools they are!") Once they have the votes, they can easily act against the interests of those people.

Social media is relatively 'democratic'. That is, you don't have to be rich to get started, and to develop an online presence, even to become an 'influencer'. People follow you, and you can decide where you want to lead them.

It takes much more money to start a newspaper, and one reason for doing so might be to influence people. The main purpose of many newspapers is not simply to report news, but to report it in such a way that benefits the newspaper owners. People buy the paper and the owner can decide where to lead them.

In both cases, influence takes priority over truth. You need to be smart to avoid being led away from honest reporting and being simply manipulated.

Before the game I

Sport is fun. It's about skill, it's often about teamwork. And it's about competition.

It's about a will to win. Against others. There are rules, otherwise there could be no game, but within the rules there can be deception. In soccer, good ball skill can deceive an opponent, and corner-kick hand signals, for example, are meant to be understood only by team-mates. A change of tactics mid-game can surprise the other side. That's one reason why half-time team talks are important – and why you don't want the other side to know what's been said.

We play with deception.

Before the game II

Or maybe before the fight. Deceit is part of the cruel human game-playing that we call war.

The Haka, originating with the Maori people of New Zealand, has become part of Rugby folklore. It's a display of confidence, eye-to-eye with the opponent. If it's intended to intimidate, it works. In a serious confrontation, not just in sport, that doesn't have to be a bad thing – a show of strength can encourage the other side to talk, or, better still, to run away, so that battlefield death is avoided.

If a fight proceeds to the stage of mutual slaughter then the display doesn't just show confidence but gives it, increasing the chance of winning and of survival.

Some events in history stand out as especially evil. One of these is the Holocaust – the murder of millions of people, mostly Jewish people, by the Nazis, because they were regarded as outsiders, or 'not us'. This is a chilling photograph, from the year 1943. Those people had just arrived at an extermination camp, in railway trucks. They didn't know it, but most of them were about to murdered – including the baby on the right.

It seems less likely to happen now, because of international journalism as well as satellites that can see details on the ground. People are less likely to commit great evil when they know they are being watched.

The evil treatment of European Jewish people was at least part of the thinking behind the formation of the state of Israel, in 1948, in Palestine. Jewish people lived in that region more than a thousand years ago. However, the creation of the new Israel displaced many of the Palestinians from their land, and those who now live in Israel do not have equal rights of citizenship. It seems that injustice breeds injustice.

An evil that is comparable to the Holocaust is the Atlantic slave trade, along with other enslavements going back through human history.

One feature of law is the belief that each individual person is responsible for his or her own behaviour. It means that unthinkingly following leaders, just 'obeying orders', is no excuse for evil actions.

But most people look around them and if they see others doing wrong, or simply not challenging wrong-doing, then they follow the crowd without thinking too hard. So it was that some people used guns and trickery to capture and cruelly mistreat other people, for money.

Should good law prevent people from shirking their individual responsibility?

Two flags, two countries, the USA and China

Is one always right and the other always wrong?

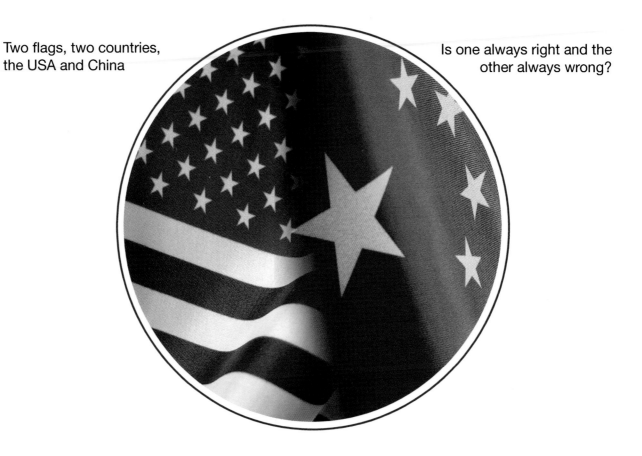

Is 'evil' something that belongs only in the past? Is the world now free of bad deeds?

Perhaps the hardest question of all is: 'what is and what is not evil?'

Different people in different places – people from different cultures – will make different judgments. In China, the great majority of people believe that their system, which has wiped out extreme poverty, but with powerful central government that can 'steer public opinion', is morally superior. In Western countries people usually believe that west is best. The West has a free press with the power, on the one hand, to 'steer public opinion' according to the wishes of the media owners, and, on the other hand, with influence that can challenge government, encourage wide debate, and sometimes expose corruption.

Disagreement about what is evil and what is not evil is a source of conflict.

Can each of us do evil by doing nothing very much? That is, by drifting on with the same old habits. Or by closing our eyes and pretending we haven't seen what's happening. Do we seek 'approval' for how we act, and fail to act, just by supposing that if others do it then it's ok? That is the unthinking approach, and it hides from personal responsibility for behaviour.

A person might have participated in the Holocaust or the slave trade, turning on the gas that was used for industrial-scale murder or putting people in chains at gunpoint. They might have justified this by, "Well, everybody else (from my culture) does it, so I can do it," or, "I was only obeying orders." Another reason that people might put forward is that, "My life is hard enough. I can't be responsible for the whole world."

Is it weak and cowardly to shirk personal responsibility for our actions and lack of actions?

Human social behaviour is not always about sweet smiles. People can irritate each other, in families, in classrooms, in workplaces. And just as we may have had temper tantrums when we were very small, most of us have experienced at least some level of anger, and person-to-person conflict.

Some quarrels pass quickly, while for some people they can last a lifetime. Getting better at managing emotions, including anger, is part of growing up.

It's comfortable to be part of a community. There are many human communities. There is comfort, familiarity and security in belonging to a particular community. That can lead those who don't examine their own thoughts and feelings too closely to a simple view: "OUR community is good, THEIR community is bad. THEY are not like us. We must build walls around OUR community, and we should treat THEM as a threat."

This behaviour occurs all over the world, and can easily lead to conflict. With conflict comes pain.

The sense of US and THEM is nothing new. And it seems that every human being still carries, either openly or hidden inside, the US and THEM feeling. Every human is capable, if they don't think enough, of believing that another human is either stupid or evil just because of their origins – such as ethnic or national origins. Racism – or xenophobia, the fear of outsiders – seems to be a common characteristic of human beings. In all parts of the world.

The Nazis in the 1940s and the slave traders before that, lived in their own worlds, and they were the ones with the guns. They thought that they could get away with their racist actions. In the modern world of communication and education, of observing and questioning the actions of the others, it's not likely to be so easy. But the potential for one group to inflict pain and death on another group is still a danger.

A nation is a community of people. It's a large one, and, unlike in many ordinary communities, everybody does not know everybody else.

Many countries have national heroes. Children are taught that they are good, with a level of 'perfection' that mere ordinary people can never reach.

Is the culture to which we give our loyalty superior to all others? Is it the centre of the world? And are outsiders always THEM, always of lower value than ourselves. Is it good that THEY are so easily demonised by 'leaders', so that THEIR defeat, even extermination, is seen as 'honourable' victory?

Can we ever rise above following leaders into 'action without thought'?

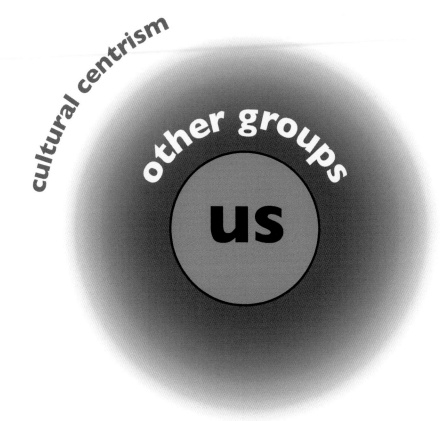

cultural centrism

other groups

us

To believe that our own culture is the superior one, the good one, is a small step on from egocentrism. It's cultural centrism.

Cultural centrism supposes that the outsiders may be evil, or it pretends that others are inferior or stupid. In some cases, arrogant people might believe that the outsiders' way of doing things is just 'misguided'. And so, from a position of supposed 'superiority' and 'righteousness', such people might want to 'help' others to be more like them. They can try to push their ways of doing things onto others.

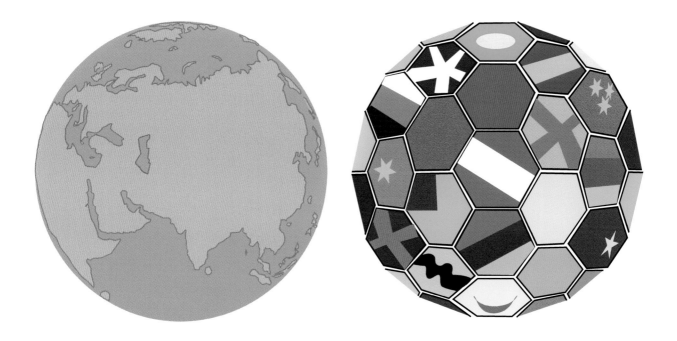

We don't just chop the world up. We add colour, with stripes, stars, moons and crosses. Why? Maybe it's just because it's the way we are?

it is hard to resist getting emotionally involved with the sports team from our own symbolled-up zone of the world. Colours and symbols provide a focus for loyalty – and loyalty puts us on the inside of the group. It gives us identity.

THEY, who are far away, are then outside the group. Some people we call leaders take merciless advantage of this, and can lead whole generations to early deaths, sometimes just to serve their own selfish needs rather than the needs of those who are sent to die.

Gunpowder was first made in China. When it first arrived in Europe there was instability and war. So the Europeans found this new explosive very useful indeed. In the end, castles became useless because their walls could be battered down in a few hours. Those seeking power had to do that in other ways, such as through politics, money, and religion. Europe became more stable. But now it had guns.

The Europeans also had another Chinese invention, compasses, which were of great help in sailing their ships far away. They met other people, who spoke different languages that they couldn't understand, had different religions, and, usually, darker skin. What they didn't have was guns.

The Europeans decided that since these new peoples were strange and less powerful (with no guns) they were inferior to themselves. So a habit grew of arrogance and self-righteousness that, in some places, has never quite gone away.

48

By any standard of judgement, some Europeans, from the main continent and from islands, behaved badly – looting, murdering and enslaving. Was it something in their DNA?

Examination of human DNA from all parts of the world shows almost no difference – and the tiny differences that do exist almost all appear on the surface, such as in skin colour. It seems that European behaviour was not a matter of DNA, but just of having better weapons at one period of history.

The ideas that one group is innately more evil than others is racism revisited.

Technology, of which guns and compasses are examples, has now spread much more evenly around the world. And education has followed. Would the just and peaceful way forward be for all to accept that every baby, new into the world, is as worthy as any other?

The horizon looks flat when we don't check very carefully. Stick two identical posts in the ground, one to the north and the other to the south, and, at the same time of day, their shadows have different length. When a ship sails off into the distance, the lower part disappears first, leaving only the upper part above the horizon.

What is beyond the ocean horizon? More ocean. Why is the faraway ocean invisible? Curvature of the Earth explains such phenomena.

It seems that we live on a ball that spins in space. It's possible to use this idea to make further predictions, such as what time the Sun will rise in Kuala Lumpur on 7th April in the year 2130. (Previous such predictions have a faultless record.)

We, humans, are not alone. There are aardvarks and zebra and many, many other things that creep and crawl, swim and fly. Some forms of life just stay where they are being importantly green, catching the energy of sunlight that drives all our lives.

We call them, all of these other living things, non-human species.

Of everything that exists on the Earth, are we the most important?

Our bodies on the inside seem to be not so different from those of aardvarks, and zebra, and chickens. Our fundamental body chemistry, so the scientists tell us, is pretty much the same as theirs.

We grow, we eat, we reproduce, we live in social groups, we die. We digest food and make waste material. So do chickens.

Despite the existence of all those other species, we are still inclined to suppose that the planet is ours, all ours. We even sometimes think that all those non-human species are ours, all ours.

So we tell ourselves that they are worthless as individuals and killing them is just fine. We are very, very good at killing – the planet's most efficient killers, by far. (It seems that T Rex had nothing on us.)

Humans do some amazing things. Singing together is just one.

We also use our voices to communicate, to work in groups, to express our feelings.

And, sometimes, we try to make sense of the world. We have a long way still to go on that. Each of us doesn't even understand our own feelings, a lot of the time. So we make mistakes. We feel hurt. We hurt others, when we don't mean to.

Still, like the planet we live on, and like distant galaxies, we are amazing. Together we are 'the big us'.

Is everything, living and non-living, here just for our benefit? Can we do what we like with the Earth and with other living things? Morally? Practically, just in terms of our own self-interest? Are we clever enough to get away with assuming that we own everything and we will always have control of nature's forces? Or do those forces control us?

We live alongside very many kinds of other living thing. Some are closely linked to us – cows, before we eat them or drink their milk, for example, or the tiny mites that eat some of the flakes of dead skin you leave behind in bed each morning.

Others would prefer no contact with us, nor we with them. We just ride on the same wondrous planet. To people, the most important living things on the planet are ... self and other people. Maybe it's the same for sharks.

us = all of humanity

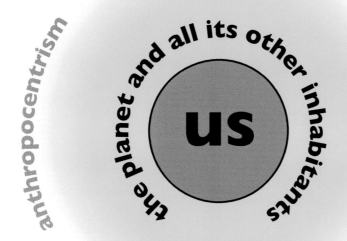

Putting humans at the centre of all existence is another centrism. ANTHROPO centrism.

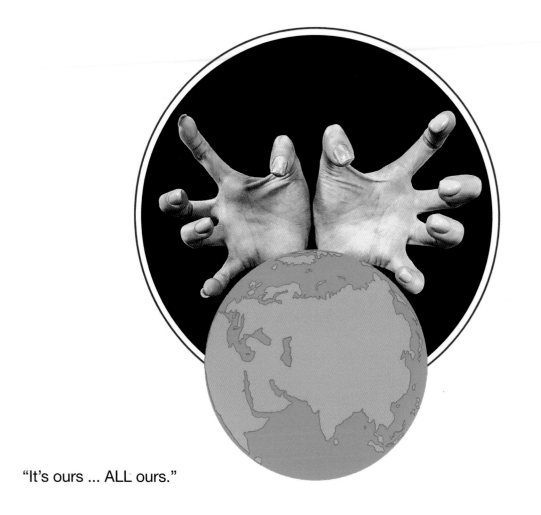

"It's ours ... ALL ours."

"We can do what we like with it."

anthropocentrism

the planet and all of its other inhabitants

us

You may, sometimes, be guilty of egocentrism. You're only human.

Sometimes your cultural centrism might come to the surface.

Are you ever anthropocentric in the way you see the world?

"O wad some Pow'r the giftie gie us
To see oursels as ithers see us!
It wad frae mony a blunder free us,
An' foolish notion ..."

Robert Burns,
Scottish poet,
written in the Scots
language, 1786

The general meaning in 'standard' English:

If some power gave us the gift to see ourselves as others see us then we wouldn't make so many blunders and we wouldn't have so many silly ideas.

We can't stand back from ourselves, "To see oursels as ithers see us!" We are stuck inside ourselves.

When we think about ourselves we are the subjects of our thoughts. We are being subjective.

It's just a little bit easier to stand back from another person, and observe, to develop a sense, or an understanding, of them.

But even then, we cannot escape from our own emotions or perceptions in any kind of interrelationship with another person. We are not free of prejudice, our own ideas that already exist, when we think about others.

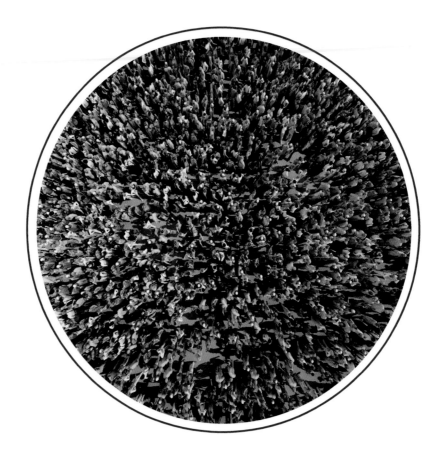

With a crowd of people that we don't know, seen from a distance, we can be more objective, as if we are on the outside. Even then, we can't break away completely, as if they were beings on another planet.

They could be people in a busy place, like a station, in which case, to us, thinking egotistically, they may be a nuisance. We can think of them as obstacles, less important than ourselves, getting in our way as we try to get on with the important things we need to do. So then we are still not detached from them. They are still wrapped up in our subjectivity.

Can we understand the world better through objectivity, through observing without emotional entanglement, or through subjectivity?

Looking at microbes through a microscope allows a high level of objectivity.

This is an approach that provides a lot of reliable (provisional) knowledge. It is one way to understand the world. But complete detachment is never possible and probably not very desirable. There is no complete escape from our world in order to look back. Objectivity has limits.

The world has many examples of opposites, that can, sometimes, seem to be in conflict.

The YinYang symbol, from ancient Chinese thinking, acknowledges these opposites and suggests that there is no overall conflict. There are just differences that create balance.

Both Yin and Yang, black and white, different but equal in importance, are necessary to form the whole, and, as shown by the curve and the dots, the boundary between them is not simple. They are entangled.

Subjective thinking and objective thinking may be forms of Yin and Yang. Only together do they form the whole.

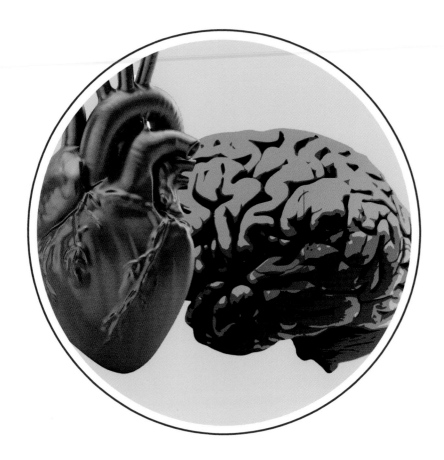

We can feel emotional pain in our chests, and strong feelings affect heartbeat. So the heart has a traditional association with emotions, while we think of the brain as the location of perception and thought.

Emotional responses and analytical responses perhaps create one example of a pair – a Yin and a Yang, together making balance.

To be objective is to stand back and examine this or that – to be detached. It can offer many new ways of seeing the world. We can gain science, and science tells us about complex ecosystems with many species of plants, animals, fungae, bed bugs, bacteria, and more.

But ... does that encourage us to forget that we live in the same world as all those other species? We need the planet's food, its water, its shelter, its space, just as they do.

We are so mixed in with other living things that it might be a good idea to remind ourselves that we cannot completely stand back from the study of ecosystems.

There are plenty more fish in the sea, they say.

There are plenty of people on the planet, too. This is bad news for fish, since we traditionally regard them as 'sources of nourishment'. By taking fish, and whatever else we can drag up from underwater, we disturb that ecosystem. The sea is part of the bigger system that includes air, rock, soil, and, of course, sunlight, and living things, so we disturb the whole world.

The disturbance could be small – at a level at which we could be just another predator, like the sharks, the orcas, and the octopuses. But our technology is clever and our social organisation allows us to be predators on an industrial scale.

This is an 'artist's impression' of the inner Solar System. It shows the Sun, Mercury, Venus and Earth. The diagonal strip of 'cloud' represents the Milky Way, far beyond the Sun and the planets.

It's not entirely false. The planets are approximately in the colours that we see when we look at them, and they are in the right order of distance from the Sun. But their sizes are hugely exaggerated relative to the distances between them.

No human has ever travelled far enough from the Earth to look back at the inner Solar System. But people have been clever enough to make predictions about motion of the planets across the sky. Those predictions turn out, by observation, to be very accurate. You can make those observations, too, if you are careful enough.

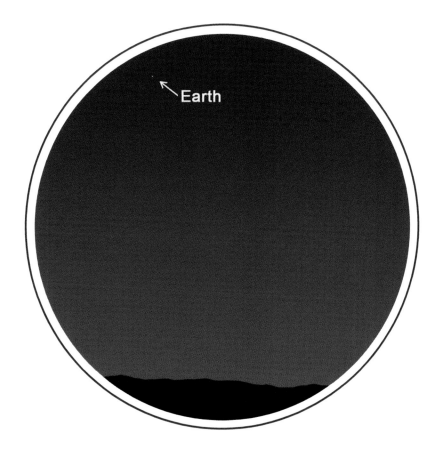

A photograph taken by the NASA Curiosity robotic rover on the surface of Mars, just after the Martian sunset at the rover's location. The image was radioed back to Earth. The small dot is our home. Earth seen from Mars looks a lot like Mars seen from Earth.

How do we know we can trust this image? How do we know we can trust NASA, the American space agency? It doesn't hurt to be sceptical. An important point, though, is that at NASA they do not work in isolation. They publish their work. Sceptical scientists in different parts of the world check their work.

The knowledge supplied by NASA may be less reliable, to you, than knowledge that you can check by your own direct observations. Less reliable is not the same thing as unreliable. You have to decide whether NASA, who are forever challenged by a global network of scientists, provide knowledge that passes your own test of 'reliable enough'.

It seems that we are not the only group of Earth's passengers that relate to the stars. Even some insects apparently use the stars to navigate, which is yet more evidence of the awesomeness of the planet.

Maybe, although we can't be sure because we don't know much about the 'thinking' of other animals, we are the only ones who look up and wonder what sort of Universe we are living in.

The planet is awesome, for sure, and that awesomeness goes on and on into the depths of the sky.

the rest of the Universe

us

anthropocentrism

geocentrism

everything else

Earth and us

Clever people in the past looked at the stars and they supposed that if we, the human species, are the most important of all the observable things that exist, then everything – the whole Universe – should revolve around us and the planet that carries us. They took a view that was both anthropocentric and geocentric – Earth-centred.

They developed elaborate mathematics to explain the pathways of other planets. They believed that such mathematics – since, they said, it could provide logical and absolute truth – was superior to knowledge from observation.

73

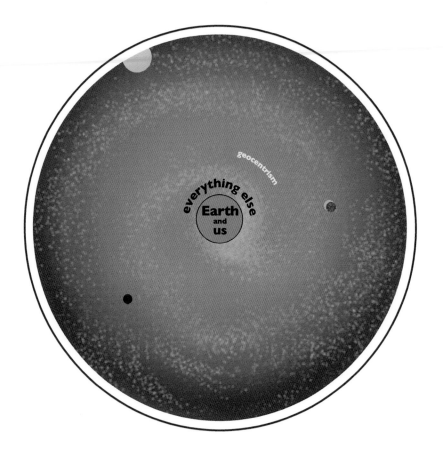

In a truly geocentric Universe, the Sun, the Moon, Mercury, Venus, Mars, Jupiter, Saturn, and all of the stars, would revolve around the Earth.

This model of the Universe, with us at the centre, was promoted as an ancient tradition by the main European church of 400 years ago. It suited their anthropocentric story.

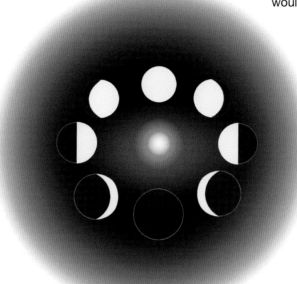

The phases of Venus, simplified as they would be seen by static observers

static observers

Actual observations are more complicated than these, which can be explained if we are not, in fact, static observers, but if we move too.

Venus, like the Moon, has phases. When we are looking at the sunny side, its reflected sunlight makes a complete circle. When the shady side is facing in our direction, it's harder to see.

Four hundred years ago, new telescopes made it possible to make careful observation of Venus and its phases. The observations were not the same as the predictions from the geocentric model of the Solar System.

This caused a lot of embarrassment, especially since a new model had already been suggested that predicted the phases of Venus much more closely. This model said that neither the Sun nor Venus revolve around the Earth, but that Earth and Venus both revolve around the Sun. Revolutionary indeed!

Not convinced? Just another story? You can see for yourself. You'll need a telescope (or good binoculars on a tripod), and you'll need to make observations over several months.

The traditional teacher passes on wisdom from long, long ago.

The teacher is Henry of Germany, the place is Bologna in Italy, and the time is about 650 years ago.

One of the reasons the new model of Sun and planets was revolutionary is that it placed direct personal observation above traditional teaching. The teacher at the front of the class was no longer the only source of knowledge – you could look for yourself.

The established authorities, who appointed themselves as the holders of truth, guardians of culture, and leaders of morality of the masses, did not like it at all.

In science, active learners can look for themselves.

The new observational science had, and has, the potential to be a subversive activity. That is, it could undermine the teaching of the authorities.

So, go on, be a revolutionary and make some direct personal observations of the world.

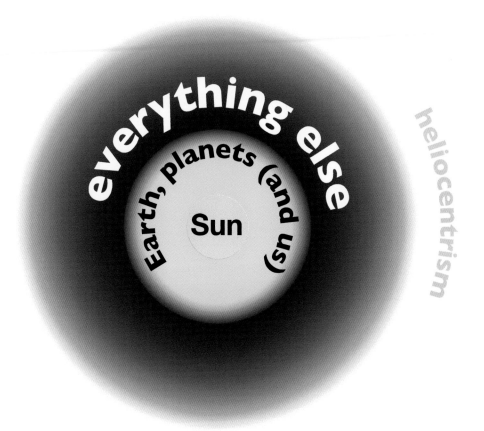

everything else

Earth, planets (and us)

Sun

heliocentrism

Observation of the phases of Venus provided evidence for the heliocentric – Sun-centred – model of the Solar System and space beyond.

If the Earth is not at the centre of everything then maybe we are not as important as we thought we were.

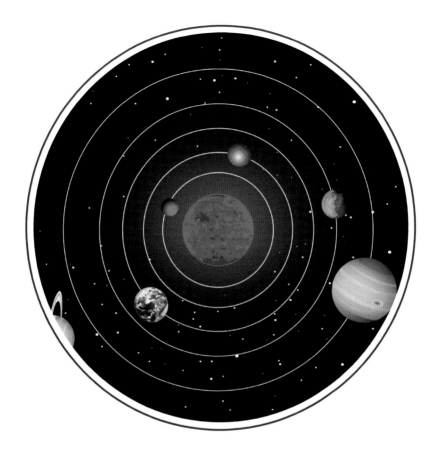

An artist's impression or 'model' of the heliocentric Solar System. It's not a lot like the real thing. But that's ok – a model stands in for the real thing. It's useful for thinking about 'reality', but it's important to remember that it is not reality.

Experience of the Sun that is more subjective.

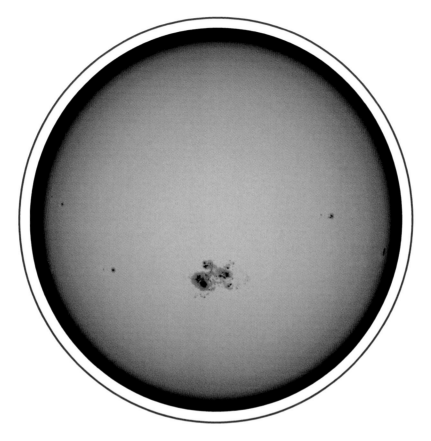

Observation of the Sun (with dark 'sunspots') that is more objective.

You don't need special equipment to see a band of light, or milkiness, across the night sky. But it helps to be in a place with little or no artificial lighting. The cloudy band is the Milky Way.

With a telescope you can see that it's a band of very many stars. If you happen to have a good telescope system you can count the stars in a small area of space, and use your answer to estimate the total number of stars in the whole band. You get an answer of about 100 billion (or 100,000,000,000) stars. Nobody knows the exact number.

You can then observe differences in how many stars there in different directions. You'll find that the stars of the Milky Way form a disk – so it looks like just a band from where we are. And you'll also see that we are inside this star collection. It seems that the Sun is one of 100,000,000,000 or more in a frisbee of suns.

There are objects other than stars in the sky. If you have good eyesight (or a good pair of glasses) and you know where to look then you can see the object in this picture, if only as a faint smudge of light. With a good telescope you can see its bright centre and its spiral shape. It looks pretty much as we reckon the Milky Way would look if we could see it from the outside. And it's a collection of huge numbers of stars. It's the Andromeda galaxy, and it seems to be not so different from our own Milky Way. With perhaps even more stars.

If you are magnificently rich you can launch a telescope into space, where it can photograph a tiny section of the sky and then radio the images back down to Earth. NASA, the American space agency, can afford to do it. They tell us that this is an image captured that way. They then explain that the bright object just above the centre of the image is a star in our own Galaxy, and its relatively close to us. Most of the other objects in that part of the sky are galaxies. And it's the same in every direction. It seems that there are billions of galaxies, each with billions of stars.

Why should we trust NASA? Are they lying to us? The next question is, why should they? They are not politicians trying to get us to vote for them. They are not companies trying to sell us anything. It's true that they need funding, and it comes from government. Having something spectacular to show helps. But if they lie then sooner or later they will lose credibility among scientists who actively look for weakness in what they say. It is not in NASA's interest to tell lies.

So just how important are you? Subjectively, looking out at the world from inside your head, you probably seem pretty important. That's fair enough – you should consider yourself to be as important as anyone else. If you don't feel that you are important then you probably won't look after yourself so well.

Objectively, you are one of more than 8 billion (8,000,000,000) people on a planet with very roughly 8 million different species of living thing, and this is one of eight planets in orbit around a Sun that is one in about 100 billion stars in the Milky Way Galaxy. And there are probably more than 100 billion galaxies.

There is a mismatch between the subjective sense of importance and the objective sense of tininess in an unbelievably vast and complex Universe. It doesn't hurt to be conscious that the whole of nature appears to be something much, much bigger than we are.

These small whitish shapes are not distant galaxies. But they are pretty much just as awesome. They are mayflies, swarming over the surface of a canal on a summer evening.

Each individual spends most of its life cycle down in the water, emerging into the air to mate and to lay eggs. Then they die. And it seems it all happens just so that the same thing can happen again next year, and the one after that, as seems to have happened millions of times, again and again, in the past.

Most human genes and mayfly genes are the same. Humans and mayflies have brains and hearts, nerve cells and muscle cells; both take in oxygen to burn food.

Alien? No, just a bee, from our own planet.

Have you looked, really looked, at nature recently. You could go face to face with a bee. Or you could check out the back of your own hand. Try curling your fingers. Make a loose fist and then relax. Why doesn't the skin split? What happens to the wrinkles of your knuckles? Observe nature. For yourself.

If you look, really look, you will never cease to be amazed at the layer upon layer of complexity. Nor at the endless beauty, from the close-up insect head all the way out to the galaxies.

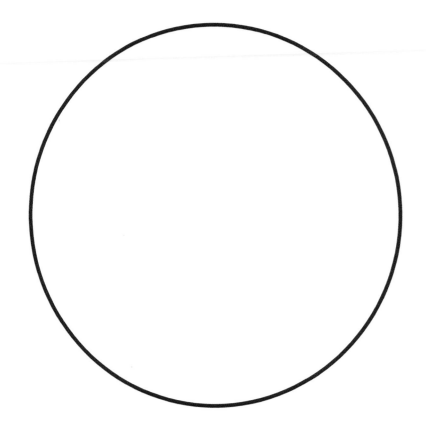

This is not the Universe. As a model of everything that seems to exists – all the complexity, all the beauty, from mayflies to galaxies – it's a bit simple.

In fact it's pretty hard to represent everything in a single graphic. But if we imagine you, me, the mayflies (and their genes) and all of the stars in all of the galaxies, inside the circle, then provided we remember that it's a model and all models are mere representations of something else, then perhaps it's not entirely useless – at least it's a good reminder that we are not clever enough to have complete model of the observable Universe.

acentrism

Human-made models may be pathetic doodles compared with the Universe, but they can help our little minds.

From looking at the Universe it seems that nowhere can be identified as the centre. It looks as if it's centre-less, or acentric.

Of course, that's current scientific thinking. A special point about science is that, being based on observation, it is not certain knowledge but only 'reliable' (or provisional) knowledge. So current thinking is not the last word. It's just the best we have so far for making sense of what we see.

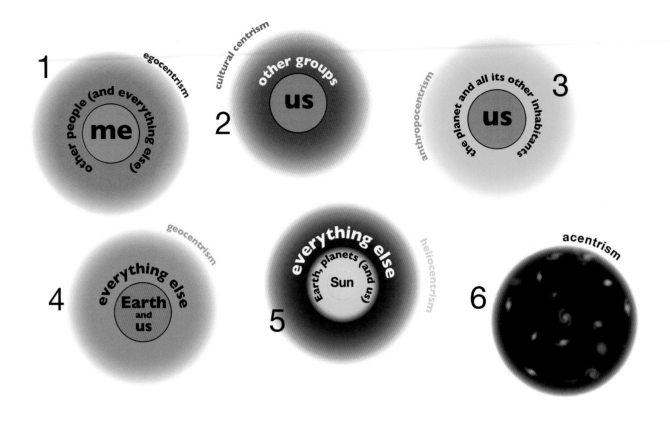

From egotism step by step to acentrism ... the sequence started with **1**, the me, me, me approach to life. It moved on to **2**, us, us, us, where our group, large or small, makes up 'us', and other people are outsiders. Even if we take an inclusive approach, so that 'we' means every human, that can leave the rest of nature on the outside, as in **3**, and can result in denial that we are part of nature. That could be a very dangerous denial.

Then, still with the arrogant supposition that we are the most important ingredient of the Universe, we can suppose that, **4**, the planet that carries us is the centre of all motion. But observation showed, **5**, that was not reliable truth. So where does that leave us, or the entire planet? It leaves us as tiny little things, curious about a world that has no centre, **6**, and still pretty much lost in the black sky, along with the aardvarks and zebra, mayflies, trees, seaweed, bacteria ...

90

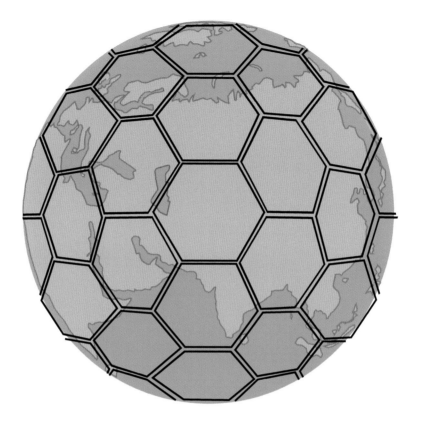

It's time to mention religion, since it is part of human life. Different societies, or cultures, and religions, originated in different parts of the world. In the past there was less contact between different places. Recently, technology has allowed more travel and communication – and different religions now speak to each other more than they once did.

But there is still that old characteristic of our species – "US good, THEM evil." Cultural centrism. "My religion is better than your religion ... na, na, ne, nah, naah." Perhaps it's not so much a problem with religion as a problem with how we are.

A clover flower, less than 2 centimetres across, growing with many others on the grassy verge of a footpath, easily passed by without taking much notice. And perhaps, soon after the photograph was taken, it was trampled on by a careless walker or an excited dog. And yet here is one part of the Universe.

With really good optical instruments you can see this – an observable, physical object just like the flower on the facing page. But bigger. It's a disintegrating star (the experts tell us) with clouds of gas bursting outwards into the space around it.

By looking carefully we can see a lot and learn a lot. But compared to the vast complexity of ... everything ... we have probably just scratched the surface of meaningful knowledge. Once we've done all of the observing and thinking that we can manage, maybe we have to be satisfied with awe and wonder.

absolute certainty	an idea that is supposed to be unable to be falsified
acentrism	the idea that the observable Universe has no centre, or that every point in the Universe has equal claim to be considered to be the centre
analysis	consideration of a problem by first breaking it down into simple parts
anthropocentrism	the idea that humans are the most important part of all that we can see
argument	a step by step approach to reach a conclusion
arrogance	the belief by a person or group that they are innately superior to others
artificial	made by people
association	a link
atheism	the idea that there are no gods or God
brain	the physical object inside animal heads
to challenge (verb)	to look for weaknesses such as untruths
common sense	the collection of ideas (assumptions) that we have on an everyday basis, without thinking too hard
community	group of people, or other species, or ecosystem
cultural centrism	the idea held by a group (community) of people that their own views and behaviours are correct and superior to those of other groups
deception (deceit)	a deliberate untruth or act of repeating untruth; deception may or may not involve malice; deceit involves malice
deferred gratification	making effort in the belief in future reward (rather than demanding immediate reward, or instant gratification)
delusion	a false idea that may be believed to be true
democracy	a form of government in which the people's interests are considered to be the most important

DNA	a long chain-like molecule that includes sections called genes
dual	with two parts
ecosystem	a network of living things and their non-living environment
egocentrism	the belief by a person that they are the most important
emotions	inner phenomena in the minds of many animals, often with outer expression shown as fear, love, or anger
entity	something that exists
equality	a state of having the same value
ethnic	relating to branches of the human species
experience	observation, or learning from observation
experiment	a deliberate act of observation; some experiments attempt to test a prediction that is based on current understanding; the experiment outcome can agree with current understanding or can falsify it; in the latter case, new ideas are needed
external world	what we suppose to be reality outside ourselves
to falsify	to show by observation that an idea is incorrect
galaxy	a body made up of very large numbers of stars
gene	a section of DNA that is passed from parents to offspring and that provides chemical templates to allow essential processes of growth and survival, such as making proteins inside cells
geocentrism	the idea that the Earth is the centre of observable existence
heliocentrism	the idea that the Sun is the centre of observable existence
Holocaust	the murder of many millions of people and an attempt to eradicate the Jewish population of Europe, carried out by the Nazis during the 1940s
humanity	the whole human population and its cultures

image	a representation of observable reality, thoughts, or emotions, usually in two dimensions
innate	existing from the origin of an entity, such as from (or before) birth of a person
interdependence	the needs of community members for others
interrelationship	connection between entities
isolation	existence without relationship to others
logic	a way of thinking that moves step by step to a conclusion, and assesses the validity of each step and of the conclusion; this works well in Mathematics, but has difficulty in providing absolute certainty when considering the observable world
social manipulation	attempts to control the behaviour of at least some of the people within a community; some news media exist for this purpose
Mathematics	the study of relationships concerning quantity and space
metaphor	use of an entity to describe another which is, in fact, quite different in most ways; example: 'This person is an angel. That person is a monster.'
Milky Way	a collection of stars that seems to be our home galaxy
mind	the collection of processes inside our heads (rather than the physical object, the brain, in which the processes seem to take place)
model	a model can be anything that shows at least some of the behaviour of something else; a fashion model stands for the customers who will wear the clothes; a model car is usually a small version; a visual model shows some (but not necessarily all) of the features of the 'something else'
moral	moral behaviour matches social expectations and normally is of benefit to the social group or community
NASA	National Aeronautics and Space Administration, the American government-funded agency that carries out flight and space research as well as space missions
nation	often also known as a country, a nation is a large community that occupies a defined area of land

nature	the observable world
objectivity	a way of understanding the world that is without emotional attachment
observation	an act of seeing (and sometimes of hearing, smelling, and so on)
optimistic	having hopeful expectations
Palestinian	relating to the country of Palestine; the country of Israel now occupies much of the original land, resulting in inevitable conflict
perception	in our minds, the organised outcome of sensing (through seeing, hearing, smelling, and so on)
pessimistic	having unhopeful expectations
philosophy	the study of ideas about what is real, what is true, what is good and what is bad
planet	a body that is too small to emit light itself, but has an independent orbit around a large light-emitter (a star)
prediction	an idea about future events
prejudice	decision-making before understanding the important information
to prove	to show to be certainly true (such as in mathematics) or show to be reliably true (such as in a court of law)
provisional knowledge	knoweldge that is believed to be true or useful based on available understanding, but may be reassessed later if there is new evidence
to publish	to make public to a wide audience
racism	different treatment of other groups of people, usually disrepectfully, based on their ethnic origins or race
to radio (verb)	to send information encoded in a certain range of electromagnetic radiation
reality	truth of what exists
religion	belief in entities, gods or God, that are worthy of worship
revolution	a turnaround of beliefs or behaviours, such as the change from the geocentric to the heliocentric models of the Universe (also known as the Copernican revolution)

Picture credits